The

SCARS

Of

RACISM

$\oplus$

Rev. Christopher D. Handy, Th. D.

This book contains the author's opinions and facts resulting from countless hours talking with people on this 'plague' that continues to invade our lives.

The author's intent is to enlighten, educate, instruct and motivate everyone to rid our society of this sore that continues to fester, and if we are not proactive, one day it will erupt.

Racism is a learned behavior. If you don't believe it, just watch little children and the way they interact before being taught by parents and others the differences between the races. For it was Jesus, the Son of God, who said that before we can get into heaven we must be as little children, that is to say humble, kind, quick to reconcile, loving, forgiving and caring.

ISBN: 1-885921-00-4   Soft-cover   12.99

Published by: **Harvest Time Publications**

PO Box 20893   **Detroit, Michigan 48220**

Dedication

⊕

To my **God** who has given me the insight to proclaim to all that it is He who made us (all people) in his likeness (Spirit). In Him, we are all one.

To my Africans our ancestors who died on the passage to America and other destinations; especially to all of those who were martyred for civil rights and the freedoms of this nation.

To all people of color everywhere who have had the misfortune of experiencing unjust and cruel treatment based solely on their race.

To those people who are representative of all races, especially the Caucasian race who are striving daily to end the horror of Racism and make the world a better place for all people.

Acknowledgments

⊕

I chose to write the acknowledgments in such a way as to include all those individuals who have influenced and shaped me. Without these persons, my life long dream of writing this book would still be just that, a dream.

My darling wife, Renita Beal Handy, who I love and care for very much. You have been the pillar of strength in my life that has kept me strong throughout the course of this project. Your keen eye and dedication as *editor* has made this work a success. I thank God daily for sending me such an intelligent, wonderful, kind hearted, loving and strong woman. May He continue to bless our family. May we grow old together.

To my wonderful children, Adia Jessnita-Uchenna, Kendra Vanessa and Kendrick, nephew and nieces, Quinton Lamar, Alisha Briana and Patrice Handy, may God continue to bless each of you. Never stop reaching for the sky.

My mother, Georgia Mae Handy, who taught me to use what I had and be honest. With these two things, I would make it in life. That piece of advice was invaluable. You sacrificed a lot for me and our family. For that I Love You, and you will always hold a special place in my heart. I thank God you are my mother.

My grandmother, Lillie Mae Handy, the backbone of the family. a strong, kind hearted, caring, giving and loving woman. Over the course of my life your invaluable advice has been a blessing. I will never forget the countless times that you sacrificed so that I could have, and I thank you for it. I thank God you are my grandmother.

Caroline, Patricia and Pamela Handy, are sisters who are special in their own way. You have been a strong inspiration in my life. I thank God for each of you. Strive for excellence and never remove your eyes off Christ. I Love you all.

To my daddy, stepmother, sisters and brother may God bless and keep you all in His loving care.

My Uncle Leroy Handy has surpassed the role that an uncle should have in his nephew's life. You were always there when I needed someone and supported my every effort. You are the man I always wanted to be, honest, trustworthy, kind, understanding, loving and a family man. I could never say in words how I felt about you so I am saying it now. Thank you and I love you uncle.

My Aunt Ivy Handy has always supported me throughout my life. Often times you treated me more like a son than a nephew. Countless times you were there for me when I needed you. Thank you and I love you very much.

Dewayne Handy is a cousin who over the years has been more like a brother and best friend. You have always been there for me and supported my every effort. I say thank you, cousin, and I love you very much.

My mother-in-law and father-in-law are two of the most wonderful people I know. You have treated me more like a son than a son-in-law. Your encouragement throughout the years has been enriching and fulfilling to me. I will always hold a special place for you in my life. I love you both very much.

My brother-in-law is a thoughtful man, who probably does not know that all my life I wanted an older brother who I would be able to talk to and share many things. Your are kind hearted and loving, and more than that you are a wonderful person. May God bless and keep you. I love you.

Logtown Baptist Church in Monroe, Louisiana is the source of my spiritual beginning outside of my family. Throughout the course of my life, various members were very supportive in my ministry and a strong symbol of family. To me that meant a lot. Thank you and I love you all each and every one of you very much.

Rev. Virgil Vandenburg, a seasoned minister who is rooted and grounded in the word of God, is my teacher, mentor, advisor and very good friend. You have truly been a blessing to me not only because of your contribution to the production of this book but to my ministry as a whole. I thank God for allowing our paths to meet. You are a God send. Thank you and I love you.

The members and friends of Hartford Memorial Baptist Church in Detroit, MI have really been a blessing to me and my family. Especially when I first relocated to the area, I did not know anyone, and you made me feel welcome and took me under your wing. People like John Taylor, Genoria Wright, Judy Simmons, Pathfinders Sunday School class, the ministerial staff and others were genuine and offered their assistance. Thanks for everything and for your prayers as God continues to use me in His service. I love you all very much.

Rev. Dr. Charles G. Adams, pastor of Hartford Memorial Baptist Church, has truly been a positive factor in my ministry. You taught me that if I trust in God and use what I

have, I can "Make Bricks Without Straw".
Thank you and God Bless You.

To my Brothers and Sisters in the ministry
at Hartford, thank you all for your friendship
and support. I love you all.

The pastor, members and friends of Bethel
Friendship Missionary Baptist Church in
Highland Park, MI are kind hearted
Christians who opened the door of the church
and allowed me to exercise my gift from God.
To the Rev. Robert L. Johnson, I will never
forget your example, and when I become
pastor, I will be as gracious to others as you
were to me. May God bless you and your
family. Thank you and I love you.

To the members of Bethel Friendship who
have become close friends you are some of the
warmest and the kindest people I know. May
God bless and enrich your lives. I truly love
each and every one of you.

To my daughter's Godparents, Jennifer
and Ralph Cannon, I thank you for your
friendship, love and support. Your
encouragement throughout this project

has made it what it is, a blessing. Thank you and I truly love both of you very much.

To Major Donald McClanahan of the Monroe Police Department in the city of Monroe, Louisiana and Chief Joseph E. Thomas of the Southfield Police Department in Southfield, Michigan I appreciated the knowledge I received from interviews with you. I was truly enlightened on the science of police work and administration. I view law enforcement with greater insight and realize that there are those who are really concerned for the people and justice. I thank you both for your time and consideration. May God Bless you.

To Cardinal Chimba Chui of the Pan-African Orthodox Christian Church and the Shrines of the Black Madonna, a deep and profound man of wisdom and knowledge. A man whose vision and concern for the well being of Africans and African Americans. Without his direction and challenge to me, this book would not be what it is, a success. May God bless you.

My doctor, Harvey P. Sabbota, D.O., his nurse, Diane, and the entire staff, were vital in the completion of this project. Your concern for my health and well being has been invaluable. Thank you very much and may God Bless you.

Margi Fizer, owner and operator of Dallas Salon in Ferndale, Michigan, is a good and kind friend who welcomed me to Michigan and was always there to offer kind and encouraging words. May God continue to bless and strengthen you and your staff. Thank you for everything.

Rubie Martin, a dear friend and spiritual sister who has been a blessing to this project. Thanks for everything, and we love you.

Foreword

The Bitter Bitter Pill

An ugly remembrance: this I will never forget. A white Assembly of God minister visited my parents home periodically over the years. One thing the minister would say every time he did visit my father's home in discussing his dealings with some man in the little town of his and my fathers town of residence. This he would say "I treated him like he was a white man."

Obviously he believed a white man deserved special consideration. One should treat a white man better and more justly than he treated an Indian, a Mexican, an African American or any of an assorted lot of minority persons.

This ignorant vacuous statement is the slogan supreme of these 50 states. Most white Americans believe that there is a "white privilege" to be associated to persons of Anglo-Saxon physical description.

White America, its institutions and its folkways have driven this lesson home to their own children. They have taught this lesson to all who live in this country.

To white America this is not an insult that injures the psyche of the citizens of this country. This shibboleth is just an unvarnished truth.

Until we have purged America's soul of the spectrum of "white privilege", this granite monolith will kill the spiritual life and virtue of this nation.

How can we expect anything other than misunderstanding, bitterness and conflict to proceed for this errant national policy of imperialism and white supremacy.

Who can drink the gall that is America?

The parable of the litter box

Every time I see a cat occupied in the covering up of what it does in its litter box, I think of America's ignoring and muffling the cries of anguish made by America's black male population. How passionately we tell the world by our conduct that we fear that his inequitable balance that disfavors black men will through some quirk change, and the powerless will be raised to a stature of equality.

Our executives and administrators at every level refuse to make either a promise or a commitment to American virtue that will strike the chains from such a large proportion of our citizens. Economic fairness is still the right of a selected few. The tease at full employment, a sub standard and unrealistic minimum wage are our "Alice In Wonderland".

Our obligation to rightness is half hearted soulless. Still we stir in the litter box.

Rev. Virgil Vandenburg

INTRODUCTION

$\oplus$

The Black experience in America has not been and probably will not be an easy one for African American people. Because of one simple fact, the color or our skin is *"Black"* when in reality African Americans skin tone ranges from pale or light hue to a chocolate brown.

My ancestors were stolen from their homes, stripped of their culture, religion, identity and families all because they were *black*. They were packed into hulls of ships and many died on the passage to America and other destinations all because they were *black*.

The great majority were separated from their families and sold on auction blocks like merchandise all because the pigment in their skin was *black*.

Our people were enslaved, and our women raped because they were *black*. Many of the African men were castrated and lynched because they were *black*. Others were murdered, denied fair and equal Justice and hated all because they were *black*.
Many were taunted, beaten and jailed because they were *black*.

Because they were Black, many of our schools and universities, businesses and churches were burned and bombed. All of this and a whole lot more horrible things were done and is being done to my people simply because our skin is BLACK.

Put all of this together and what do you have? One giant wound deeply embedded into the souls of African American people. Due to the neglect and uncaring concern from society to properly tend to this wound, a scar has formed which has created a barrier in the advancement of African American people in this nation.

But the time has truly come for a healing to remove this visible unsightly wound in the souls of African Americans. It is going to take all of us united together in brotherly love. Love is needed now to allow the scars to be covered forever. This will not be an overnight process; it will take some time. The Bible says that time heals all things, all wounds... Thank God for Time.

"... A time to kill, and a time to heal; a time to break down, and a time to build up;"
Ecclesiastes 3:3

Contents

Chapter 1

⊕

Racism

"What is RACISM?"

After much intense research, I have come to the final conclusion that there is no dictionary, no encyclopedia, no commentary or any book of my knowledge that could ever describe the deeper meaning of racism.

First of all, it is a learned behavior taught by parents and others to their children. It is their belief in the superiority of one race over another or others. It is intensified to the point of forcing one's culture and way of life upon the other ethnic groups, while at the same time expressing inferiority toward other races.

Racism to an African American is a pain so great that it reaches deep within one's soul and hurts that individual so much so until it causes a spiritual scar. A scar that never completely heals or goes away because it is always reopened by the nasty, vicious instrument of racism.

Consequently, at the hands of a Godless dominant group of people, the victim suffers severely by physical, emotional, economical, social and political means.

Therefore the victimized race is deprived of all the freedoms, privileges, and other advantages that life and this country have to offer.

In order to truly understand this statement, one must look at RACISM from all aspects... physically, emotionally, economically, socially and politically.

Physical Means:

These Godless persons who consider themselves superior would use any means necessary to destroy the ones they consider inferior. They would go to the very extreme of introducing harmful and addictive drugs, debilitating alcohol and dangerous weapons into certain communities so that the people may destroy one another or themselves in the process of destroying his fellow man.

Poor and innocent men and women are being set up, beaten, jailed and even killed by a majority of racist cops. Whereas these same cops, whose salaries are paid with our tax dollars, have no regard for the lives of many ethnic groups, especially African Americans. They feel that all must perish if considered a threat to their existence.

Frankly, I see why the 'Lady of Justice' wears a blindfold over her eyes. Even though she may not see the injustices being done, she cannot avoid hearing the

cries and moans of people being
oppressed by a wicked and evil devil that
is murdering thousands and thousands of
my people everyday through the deceitful
means of drugs, alcohol, weapons that
are being smuggled into black and other
neighborhoods across this country.
By this means many die a death so
horrible that it could be called Genocide.

        "Wake Up My Brother and Sisters and
LIVE !!"

Emotional means:

     During the African American exile here
to the this strange land called America,
my and many other ancestors were stolen
from their homeland, stripped of their
culture, identity, language and religion
and brought here to be slaves and to be
dehumanized, ill-treated, slaughtered,
castrated, raped and

lynched simply because of the color of their skin and the upper hand the oppressor had at the time. Therefore, nothing could ever erase the emotional *scar* that has severed the spirit of the African American people.

When the oppressor could no longer kill them, he then resorted to killing the inner spirit of the people. The Godless oppressor knew that if he could break the spirit of the people, then he had in effect killed the people. Becuase if you can kill the spirit of any people, you have complete control and have destroyed their will to survive, their will to progress, their will to stand up and be counted.

Consequently, by treating him like less than nothing, you could lower them to a state of nothingness. In the eyes of the oppressor, he sees the one being oppressed as nothing and after a while the one being oppressed starts to believe that he (or she) is nothing and starts acting like nothing.

Likewise, the Spiritual destruction of a beautiful people dies.

With the one true God being the only hope for a resurrection, only then can the oppressed be restored to being greater than they could ever imagine.

Glory be to the one true God.

Economic means:

One of the most important factors in securing our freedom from the white oppressor's control is through various economical means. If African Americans are able to obtain the much needed economic advantage not to compete but turn the tables on the oppressor then we would not have to depend on the oppressor to 'throw a bone every now and then'.

While the oppressor is in control of much of the money, the great majority of African American people suffer severely. When the oppressor decides to cut funds targeted for the poor and needy, namely African American, black colleges close, and much needed programs which are geared toward the poor, disadvantaged and inner city children are no longer able to operate due to the lack of funds.

He (the oppressor) responds by saying there is no money for these programs. But at the same time, more jails and prisons are being built and billions are spent on the Nations Defense Fund.

He gives money to foreign governments as loans knowing all along that many of those same governments will never pay it back. He even gives loans and a Tax free seven (7) year period to foreigners who come into this country applying for citizenship.

Likewise, my people, African Americans, who have been here for over 400 years, cannot get a loan of any type whereby they are able to advance by owning their own businesses and becoming self sufficient. When they cannot obtain financial capital, the oppressor labels them as unreliable, a risk.

How wonderful it would be if we could be in control of our own money and economy. We would be able to support our own colleges, medical care programs, trade schools and special programs for the poor and needy.

We would start our very own business corporations, build our own banks, shopping malls, airlines, hotels and much more. We can do all of this ourselves and keep our dignity without changing our positions on a matter or distancing ourselves from a certain person or group simply because their views may offend those who are currently in control of their financial resources.

If we are in control, we can associate ourselves with whom ever we decide. In retrospect the Million Man March, which was an extraordinary event that history will never forget, purposed some wonderful ideas. One of which was that if African Americans would put their resources together, we would have billions to do for ourselves.

Buying business and communication corporations, building our own schools and universities, organizing our own Medicare system, starting our own banks, investing in our own communities can all be done if we obligate ourselves to a mere $10 a week, and if one hundred thousand people were to commit themselves to this pledge in one year, we would have $52,000,000.

Just imagine what 200,000, 300,000 or even a million people could do if they committed themselves to this wonderful task. We could have billions within one year, and we (African Americans) would be in total control as to how this money would be spent.

The choice is ours; a bone thrown to you by the oppressor at his leisure or unite together and share in economic freedom and become self sufficient.

A bone or freedom, the choice is ours; win together in unity or lose in division.

Social means:

History has taught us that if you are remotely different from society or in the eyes of the oppressor, you are considered to be an outcast from society. In Bible times if you were a gentile (any person who was not a Jew and much later a Christian), you lived in the mountains, far, far away from the Jews who considered themselves to be above all.

In American History, the oppressor took the beautiful and rich lands of the Indians and forced them to move to reservations far away from civilization so that they would not have to socialize with them. The same occurred in the history of African Americans; in the days of slavery, we had no land or property that could be taken just our bodies, spirit and minds.

During the civil rights era, visible and invisible signs were used to dictate where African Americans then called 'Colored' could and could not go. If you were allowed in certain businesses, you had a special door to enter, certain areas to sit or stand, eat or be served. There were certain hospitals that only treated Black people, separate schools, riding in back of the bus, even drinking from separate water fountains and using different restrooms.

Society has not changed much from those days. We(African Americans) still are not accepted by society who tend to see us an 'invisible people', unrecognized as a people who are unaccustomed to the freedoms, justices, and opportunities of this society, underrated and destined to fail at any and everything attempted.

The African American worst enemy is the media. It constantly portrays the negative side of African Americans and rarely the positive side. As long as the oppressor controls the media, the African American social status will never change for the better. Until we are in control of the media (that is to say own more and more communication broadcasting companies) where we will be able to display a truthful image of ourselves as we know and see ourselves.

Political means:

One thing that we as African American fail to utilize is our power of the vote. History tells us how so many of our people were jailed, beaten, bitten by dogs, sprayed by huge water hoses, lynched, bombed and maliciously murdered so that this and other generations could have the right to vote and to have their voices heard. Yet many of us do not exercise that right.

Consequently, the oppressor is able to get into power, and once in power, he then cuts funds of much needed programs for the youth, poor and needy. Also, he (or she) creates laws of injustice that are focused on African American males and females. Lastly, there is always a bill or push to eliminate Affirmative Action; ending this practice of placing very qualified minority persons into positions is the prize the oppressor seeks daily. When we do not VOTE, we are helping him to hurt us.

We have the power to put those persons into office whom we feel have the integrity and who are capable to get things done. Especially those things that are needed in the Black and other minority communities.

We have the power to elect a Congress and a President of our choice. We also have the power to remove those individuals from office who do not meet our agenda. We have the power at our fingertips to make the necessary changes in our political arena.

When we support a Black candidate, who is qualified for the office or position in which they seek and meets our agenda, we should support them whole hearted not only with our votes but also with our money. It takes money to run and operate a campaign.

Therefore, we must rally behind our candidates during the election and especially after the election. Special funds should be set up for candidates to help them in the campaign.

Local churches, Black organizations, clubs, etc. should unite to help them in their bid for public office. So great men like Rep. Cleo Fields of Louisiana could get their message out in order to draw support.

In my opinion, he would have made an excellent governor. He was honest and sincere, and most of all he cared. Louisiana lost a saint and ended up with a less qualified individual.

The choice is ours as to what we do with our voting power, use it wisely or abuse it. We as African American can control our own destiny. We must remember and never forget all of those who died wishing for the opportunity to VOTE.

Vote! Too many lives depended on it.

Chapter 2

⊕

Racism in Religion and World History

"Crippling the Truth"

I could not write this book on racism without adding my two cents worth of knowledge on racism in Religion and World History. In many Black churches today, there are pictures hanging in them that portray a lie which cripples our youth and blinds our older generation. What is the lie? The picture of a White (Caucasian), blue eyed, long blond hair man, whom the Euro-centric white Religion leaders and scholars say is Jesus Christ, the Son of God.

For years I believed the lie that Christ was a white man and all of the characters in the Bible were all white men. I thought the few mentions of black people were in Genesis, where Noah's son Ham was cursed to be Black and to serve all mankind. Secondly, in Exodus 2, the wife of Moses, who was named Zipporah, was Black, and thirdly as found in St. Luke 23:26, Simon, a Cyrenian, who carried Christ's cross.

Those were the only references to the Black presence in the Bible that were given to me as a child. However, when I grew up, after much research and careful studying, I discovered many African American scholars who have challenged the white Eruo-centric interpretation of the Bible.

These wonderful beautiful Black people whom I will not name due to the fact that I may slight the extraordinary talents of these gentlemen and women who have removed the scales from our eyes. So I will refer to them as beautiful, God gifted and talented Black people.

These God gifted people have taken on the challenge to educate our people and inform the world of our true presence in the Bible and World History. Black people were the first race of people to ever walk the Earth, first to build civilizations, first to set up institutions of learning, develop hospitals and invent various forms of medicine, great architects who constructed huge structures and pyramids that are still standing today.

To the world it seems a mystery as to who had the foresight and how the plans were designed and executed to create these structures. There are even those who know the truth about the presence of Black people in world History, yet still refuse to acknowledge their amazing accomplishments and to give credit where credit is due.

In order for the truth to be told and told correctly, we as African Americans must accept the challenge to first educate not only our children but also the older generation. We must teach the importance our race played in Bible and World History.

First we must begin in the home by reading books about Black History and African American accomplishments. We must continue to instill confidence and purpose into our young children, remove all false images that reflect a white God and teach the truth about Jesus Christ's origin.   The fact is He was born and reared in a region where the people were black.

Secondly, our churches must set up Bible classes, Sunday School classes and other church programs so that our African culture, especially the presence in the Bible, may be expressed and taught. Pastors, Ministers, Laymen, Sunday School teachers, Deacons and others who play an important role in the educational operation of the church should take a class in African History so they will be able to preach and teach the truth about our presence in the Bible.

This way we will no longer have to rely on others to tell us our own history. We will be capable of distinguishing and discussing our own history. We will no longer live in total darkness to the truth of our existence.

Thirdly, we as parents, guardians and concerned individuals should re-instate our African traditions of passing down our history through story telling (the Griot). We must demand that more of our schools give our children a class in African and African- American History whereby they can be taught concrete and positive facts of their own history and heritage. A history that this world and society have tried for so long unsuccessfully to hide, cover up and even destroy.

But we as African Americans have God on our side who will not allow the truth to be denied from his people. The more they try to cover it up, the more it becomes uncovered.

In closing, I would like to leave this final thought to all African Americans. We have a beautiful and incredible history that began long before anyone ever starting writing history. It tells of a people who like you and me were and are still incredible, strong and courageous.

Our history which is so unique that it tells of a great beautiful Black people that lived centuries ago. Our ancestors, when in Africa, built great beautiful kingdoms, powerful armies and a government that worked.

These kingdoms were ruled by strong, wise black kings and queens who were able to instill faith, purpose and determination into their people. Our history tells us of the many inventions that we contributed to the world and especially to this country with little or no credit going to African community for their valuable contributions.

Without knowing the true history of people, there lies no identity or mission; therefore, no liberation can ever come for that race of people, only a mystery surrounds their past and future, thus leaving them in a state of unconsciousness.

One more important aspect about our true history that cannot be denied, is that the vast majority of black people are truly spiritual and are on the very pulse of God. This is how close we are to God. They (oppressor) may erase the black from our skin, but never the God from our hearts.

God has always played an important role in the lives of black people. All the way to the beginning of time and to the present. If things are to ever get better for black people, we must return back to our Faith in God where by we may unite together in brotherly love and brotherhood.

We are a black people (African Americans) have nothing in which to be ashamed. God made no mistakes when He made the black race. We are rich with history, rich with a God that will always be with us and always on our side. After the Lord God had finished his creation of the Earth, he ended with this beautiful word "GOOD".

Black has been and will always be "GOOD". Despite what history or society may say or think. We must thank God for our wonderful history and for our beautiful history and for our beautiful race.

Chapter 3

⊕

Black Against Black
"The Willie Lynch Syndrome"

It amazes me quite often to see the strength and unity that other races of people seem to possess.   They have family   unity,   community   unity,   and cultural unity.   They work and strive together for the good of their people. They *bond* together whenever they are threatened by an outside force and remain   unified until victory is won or justice is served.

Another thing   that I observe is that they are a proud people, proud of their culture, developments, accomplishments, and most of all they encourage one another to also strive and excel in whatever task they undertake. For that same reason, I believe that is why they remain unified and strong.

For the majority of my people, the African American, it is the opposite. We are so divided that one could place an entire universe between us and that would not be enough to bridge the gap that separates African Americans.

This could only display the extent of serious problems that African Americans are having with one another.

In conjunction we refuse to help our own, support our black owned businesses, support our black political candidates, even black schools and colleges that promote the well being of African Americans as a whole.

Some blacks have even gone to the extreme to denounce their own blackness. This is called anti-black or "the Clarence Thomas syndrome" (those who are against anything that is black or associated with being black). They have begun attacking all blacks in general. On the other hand, many blacks are constantly killing and destroying the very lives of their own people through drugs and violence. Our people (African American) have become some of the heartless people on this planet with no regards for human life or the preservation of life. Nor are they concerned for saving their race from total genocidal annihilation from the oppression.

I have come across some African Americans in stores, malls, on the streets, or even in church who just refuse to communicate (speak) to one another or even look directly at one another. It seems to me that they literally hate me for being who I am... Black.

One would think by working under some black supervisors or managers, things would be a little better on the job. Wrong, they sometimes are worse; They feel that they have something to prove;

therefore, they will be seen as one in authority.

To have your own people hate and mistreat you without a cause or reason is a betrayal against our one true God, our ancestors who died so we may be united as one) and most of all against one another. Now, especially during these difficult times, we need the strength, wisdom, and courage of one another to unify ourselves.

Question: Where and how did all of this begin?

In 1712, on the banks of the James River, a white plantation owner from the West Indies by the name of Willie Lynch spoke to a crowd of slave owners from the colony of Virginia regarding the problems that they were having with their slaves. Willie Lynch stated in his speech that you do not have to hang or torture your slaves in order to keep under control.

He said that it was a waste of valuable stock. He said, "Here is my bag, I have a fool-proof method for controlling your black slaves. I guarantee everyone of you that if installed correctly, it will control the slaves for at least 300 years."

He also goes on to say that it is a simple method and members of your family or any overseer can use it. He states that he outlined the number of differences among the slaves and after he did that, he would take these differences and make them bigger.

He uses fear, distrust and envy for control purposes. He assured the crowd that distrust is stronger than trust, and envy is stronger than adulation, respect or admiration. He urged each plantation owner to take this simple list of differences and think about them.

On his list of differences was age, color (or shade of skin), intelligence, size, sex, size of plantation that they are on, status of plantation (profitable or non-profitable), attitude of owner, where the slave lives (on a hill, east, west, north or south), texture of hair (do they have fine hair or coarse hair), height (tall or short). One more important thing that you should never forget to do that is to pitch the old black slave against the young black slave, and the young black slave against the old black slave.

Also, do pitch the dark skin slaves against light skin slaves and the light skin slaves against the dark skin slaves. The black slave after receiving this indoctrination shall carry on and will become self-refueling and self-generating for hundreds of years, maybe even thousands of years.

Lastly, he states, "You must also have your white servants and overseers distrust all blacks, but it is necessary they trust white servants and overseers and depend on us. They must love, respect, and trust only us. Have your wives and children use these methods and never miss an opportunity. My plan is guaranteed to work. It worked on my modest plantation in the West Indies, and It will work through the South and the world."

Nearly three hundred years later, this plan that Willie Lynch introduced in 1712 is still apparent among African Americans today. I call this attitude 'The Willie Lynch Syndrome'. From that kind of mentality we get the <u>Clarence Thomas's</u> and the <u>Uncle Toms</u> , those who hurt or destroy their own people so that they will be able to keep in favor with the Oppressor so they can get ahead.

Anti-blacks are those who denounce their blackness, culture, religion and all that has associated them with being Black. Some consider themselves as highly sophisticated, BUPPY and snobbish and better than other blacks because of education, financial status, job status, residence, organizations in which they are affiliated, etc.

Now we have come to the primary cause of our division as African American people, what is our solution to this problem?

My Cure for "the Willie Lynch Syndrome:

Step 1   ATONE!

We must atone (make amend and repent) ourselves as we black men did on October 16, 1995 in Washington, D.C. at the Million Man March. But now is the time that all black people , men, women and children everywhere needs to atone themselves.

Ask God to come in and create within us a clean heart and mind that we may not harbor any malice, envy or hatred towards one another and remove the scales from our weary eyes so we may view our beautiful black brothers and sisters not as things to be used, abused, forsaken, and destroyed, but the way our one true God intended for us to view them as sons and daughters of the Almighty and also as our brothers and sisters who have been taken from us through deceit.

The one true God has brought us together. As long as we keep God in the midst, we will always be unified together.

Step 2   Love - Compassion

I am reminded of a beautiful song I once heard sung titled "What the World Needs Now is Love, Sweet Love." What African Americans need most in their lives to unify them is simply Love.

Love is the one important element missing from our lives and our relationships with one another. We rather hate than to love because hate does not require anything in return.

But love requires us to be accountable. You cannot love in words only, but you must love in deeds, actions and good works towards your fellow man.

Black people for so long have been taught by the oppressor to hate their fellow black brothers and sisters. The oppressor felt that if he could place hate between blacks, then his plan of separation had worked.

This is a new day and with that new day brings a shower of Love. Love that can close any size gap that separates us as a people and unifies us as a whole. Love changes things, and Love can unlock any door that has been sealed by the 'Willie Lynch Syndrome'.

Step 3   Trust

We must began to trust one another in all circumstances. We as a people have never been able to truly trust fully our

black brothers and sisters. Whereby we
can put our total confidence in them.

This trust is lacking in our
communities, homes and churches. The
main reason why many of us refuse to
trust our race is because they have been
hurt, deceived, betrayed, and forsakened
by the very people of their own race. So it
is very difficult to trust anyone after you
have been victimized by them.

So a new relationship must began first
with God and then with your black
brothers and sisters. Through that
relationship a bond must be established
whereby trust can enter and abide. From
our present status, we must began to
trust our black brothers and sisters.

Because we can trust God with all of
our hearts, soul and mind, surely we can
trust our black brothers and sisters.
Trust is essential with our relationships
with one another and our survival as a
people.

Step 4   Build

The Willie Lynch Syndrome for years, decades and even centuries has done nothing but destroy the lives, unity and spirit of African American people. It was the most horrible plan that ever was inflicted against African American people.

It did everything in which it was designed. Turing the old against the young, young against the old, dark skin against the light skin blacks, light skin blacks against the dark skin blacks, coarse hair blacks against fine hair blacks and so on.

We need to put all of that grief behind us now. It is a new day; the day of Jubilee, a new beginning for all of us. African Americans must prepare to build on that solid foundation of hope, atonement, love and trust.

If we have hope then we are able to foresee a bright and better future for all blacks, African Americans , and all people, despite all of the obstacles that have been placed in our way. I am reminded of a passage of scripture from the Bible (RSV) in the Old Testament , the book of Nehemiah,

Nehemiah Chapter 2: Verses 17 - 18.

Then I said to them, "You see the trouble we are in, how Jerusalem lies in ruins with its gates burned. Come let us build the walls of Jerusalem, that we may no longer suffer disgrace.

And I told them of the hand of my God which had been upon me for good and also of the words which the king had spoken to me. And they (the people) said "Let up rise up and build". So they strengthend their hands for the good work.

After the people realized their troubles, they then began to realize it was time to build. So they responded by saying, "Let us rise up and build". We too can respond in the same such manner as Israel did. Whereas a people who posses hope will have no limitations as to what they can accomplish. I myself shall always and forever remain a prisoner of hope.

Let us apply these steps and bring about an immediate death to the 'Willie Lynch Syndrome' once and for all. In my closing, I would like to say that the time has come for us as a people to rise up from our devastation and began a new day whereby our future will be crystal clear and have a long life.

So, when the people of the future look back to this time, they will say with admiration that there lived a strong, unified black people who accomplished so much in so little time. May the one true God of all bless and keep us all.
Keep Hope ALIVE!

Chapter 4

⊕

The Million Man March

"One in a Million"

On October 16, 1995, a strange event occurred in the Nation's Capitol of Washington, D.C. It was the gathering of over one million and 200,000 African American men. They came from all parts of this nation and many parts of the world, from all walks of life, Christians, Non-believers, Muslims, Catholics and many more.

There were Blue collar workers and White collar workers, and then there were no collar workers. Every occupation that you could imagine was there that day. Then there were those who had no job nor income; yet, they still came to the gathering.

These brothers (men) came together on this spot in Washington where over four hundred years earlier their ancestors were stolen from their homes, stripped of their Culture and Language and sold on this spot as slaves. On that day while our ancestors looked down from heaven, they could only smile with gladness. For their children, finally united in brotherhood and brotherly love, have come to the realization that it takes all of us united together in brotherhood, brotherly love, strength and purpose.

For too long we as a people have been divided for no good reason. Division has damaged us severely. As a whole, it has hampered our progress, stalled our means to be self supportive, and killed our obligation to support one another in business, politics or whatever else is geared toward our people.

Division never helped anyone but the enemy (oppressor). For the oppressor gets joy out of watching us at each other's throats. Because he knows that as long as we are divided, we will never progress.

At the Million Man March, many African-American males as well as myself recognized the need for unity. For with unity so much can be accomplished and gained by uniting together. The march demonstrated a strong spirit of unity that could not be suppressed by anyone.

When this nation turned on their television sets, they saw what a united body of strong black men could do and will do once they realized the importance of the purpose: God, the individual person, dignity, community, family, and people.

II

It was a day for the Black man and woman to take responsibility for their lives, to rededicate themselves back to the one true God, the creator of us all.

It was the awesome power of God that touched a nerve in this nation, that revitalized the consciousness of the Black man so that he may see himself and the importance to atone himself.

God allowed him to see himself and not see himself. With different eyes than before, the African-American man saw himself as a "new" and different person. He saw potentials and abilities. He never realized that he possessed skills that he never knew he had. He also realized that he has possessed a great deal of intelligence.

He further saw himself as a leader in his community and church, head of a household, husband to his wife, father to his children despite all else he saw a proud changed Black Man.

He did not see himself as the media, Hollywood or Television portrayed him: as a savage beast, a maniac, a baby maker who does not live up to his responsibility, a drug pusher or addict, a pimp, a killer or murderer of his own people and others, a dumb illiterate, lazy, worthless nigger. No, he did not see himself in that negative aspect; a lie that has haunted him since his existence.

On that day around the 1.2 million African-American men, the media saw no drug dealers or addicts, no savage beasts, no killers or murderers, no more absent fathers, no maniacs and he did not see any lazy, worthless Niggers.

What the world saw was a beautiful, peaceful sea of Blackness which embodied brotherly love. A sea not of water, but atoned, rededicated, strong male humans of African decent.

It was a breathtaking experience that everytime I think about it or talk about it, I become choked up and when I am alone I shed a few tears, (optional words: tears of the spiritual renewal) .

The Million Man march is an experience that I will never get over for as long as I live. I foresee a strong bright future for the Black man, the Black woman, this nation and the world.

III

The Million Man March has impacted the Black man and woman to make sweeping changes in their lives, homes, community, church, toward each other and toward all people. I do believe that progress is on the way, and the spirit of the Million Man March will live on in each of us. Thank God for the Million Man March.   Thank God for the next one.

"Long Live the Spirit of the Million Man March"

Another perspective:

Following are excerpts from another brother's account of the Million Man March (MMM)

Bro. Ralph 2X
Boston, MA

As a member of the Nation of Islam, we worked tirelessly in the Boston area for over a year pushing the MMM. Though we had some insight of the vision put forth by The Honorable Minister Louis Farrakan, we had a great deal more hope than any concrete expectation. We didn't know what to expect!

The affair was definitely led by a mighty God whose Spirit overwhelmed everyone involved. I was very much trying to be the professional and not display much emotions, but nonetheless I found myself frequently wiping tears from my eyes. Brothers on their knees praying, brothers hugging one another, greeting each other, assisting each other, and above all inspired to do more for their communities and family than they were presently doing. There were no strangers at this event... It was a Family affair. Indeed we all were VIPs.

There were no minor players, nor were there major players, a hierarchy did not exist on this day we were all on one accord. Many notable "VIP's" who were in attendance made themselves of no reputation and sought only to remain among the brothers on the Mall in unity.

When the Leader of The Nation of Islam approached the podium under the thunderous chants of , "Farrakan, Farrakhan, Farrakhan!", as the man of God he is affirmed. "To God Be the Glory!".

When I attended high school, the blacks used to make mockery of certain words and the way they were used by Caucasians. One of the words was awesome. Awesome was always perceived by us to be a white thing, that is to say 'awesome dude'; it most definitely wasn't in our vocabulary. Though after being asked to sum up my experience at the MMM, that word awesome is the first thing to come to mind. Finally, (I) have something to associate with that word.

May Allah (GOD) Bless us to maintain the Spirit of the Million Man March

Chapter 5

⊕

The Simpson Trial "Justice vs. The Media"

On October 3, 1995, the world along with myself sat in front of the television set and listened to radios, watching and waiting for the verdict of O.J. Simpson, a Black man accused of murdering his ex-wife and her friend who were both White. When the verdict was read not guilty on both counts, I cheered with joy and shouted, "Thank You, Jesus!, Thank You, Jesus!" *I did this not because two people were brutally murdered, God forbid, but because for a few short moments, we as African American people saw Justice, a missing symbol of freedom for us, the African American.*

Justice is something that many African American people do not see or experience. Prior to being accused of any crime, we are already labeled guilty.

Whenever we enter a store or other business establishment, automatically store clerks or store detectives follow and watch us closely as we walk through the business as though we intend on committing a theft or causing trouble. Whenever we present a check or credit card, we are regarded with suspicion, like our intent is to defraud.

When we apply for a job or loan, we are thoroughly investigated and re-investigated. Then we are put through a magnifying glass in search of something that may have been missed in the investigations.

There are countless African American males and females who are falsely incarcerated in jails and prisons by an un-just Justice system. O.J. was blessed to have the finances to hire expert attorneys, DNA experts, pathologists, and investigators to help him get to the truth. He was then able to fight the system on its own ground and weapon. It is said that if you have the money, you have the power; No money, No power, No Justice.

So without the adequate finances to hire good attorneys, many innocent African Americans are deprived of their constitutional rights and are jailed or imprisoned. So O.J. fought this un-Justice system. Despite the stumbling blocks that were placed in his path, he proved his innocence, and yet there is one more Jury he must convince, the Media.

It is the same Jury that all famous, outspoken, powerful, and wealthy African Americans must encounter in this country. In essence, the media can make you or break you.

All through the trial, the news media portrayed only the negative aspects of Simpson and his attorneys.

They conveniently left out the racist cop who planted evidence and did not focus on the prosecution team who did not focus their investigation on other suspects.

They did not do a thorough investigation of the ex-wife's life or her friend's. Yet O.J. Simpson's life was taken apart like a jigsaw puzzle. Every aspect of this man's life was examined, re-examined and then placed under a magnifying glass so the experts could examine him once again. This trial is said to be the "Trial of the Century" The question is why?

First of all, it consisted of a Black man, a White blond hair woman, and a White Jewish man. The Black man was accused of killing both of them. Indeed, It was reported that O.J. and his wife had marital disagreements in the past in which the police was called to settle the matter. So the police had knowledge of this matter before hand.

Secondly the Black man, O.J. Simpson, is famous and is known throughout the world. At one time, he was quite rich and considered by some to be a millionaire and powerful.

In some cases, some thought of him as untouchable. So the White media pieced all this together and initiated a trail of their own, and before the Justice system (Jury) handed down their verdict, the white media handed down their verdict, Guilty. Before all of the evidence was in, O.J. Simpson was guilty, tried and convicted of murdering his ex-wife and her friend.

An African American can never actually receive true Justice as long as the white media plays a part in the portrayal of African American people.

We have been and still are stereotyped in movies and TV shows as thugs, gangsters, drug dealers and savage killers. That image is then accepted by the American people an the world as the attitude and the behavior of African American people. Fair and equal Justice can never come to African Americans as long as the media stereotypes us and portray the negative aspects that people are so used to seeing.

In order for this society to change its hostile attitude towards the images that are portrayed, the media must change its attitude of African American people. They must change and start making more movies and television shows that portray the positive side of our race; we are loving, caring and industrious people that are used to working hard because we have great pride in who we are and whose we are, children of God.

Until steps like these are achieved in our society, there will and can never be equality in our Justice system for African American people or any other race of people that is considered to be a minority by this society.

In conclusion, true and equal Justice can only come from God almighty whose mercy endures forever.

Those who are in control of this Justice system must allow God to come into their hearts, minds and souls so that real Justice can truly be administered to all races of people. Whereby people will not lose total confidence in the judicial system, especially those law enforcement agencies who enforce it. Then and only then will there be ...

'Fair and Equal Justice For All'.

Chapter 6

⊕

The Healing Process

"Where do We Begin?"

With the rise of racial prejudice in this country, we the people of color are faced with the ongoing challenge to bring about ourselves a social change to this social injustice we face on a day to day bases. For this reason we can no longer rely on others who are not moved by compassion and who are unconcerned for our well being to solve the problems that accompany racism.

Now the time has come for all people of color to accept the responsibility to control their own destiny. First, we must begin to educate ourselves and one another so that we may begin to re-discover, in-depth, each others differences such as culture, religion and beliefs.

Secondly, we can begin the process of communication which is the key to a successful relationship that will bridge the gap between the races.

Only then are we able to share our ideas and experiences concerning the ongoing problem of racism. We must be open minded and totally honest with our feelings, when we come to discuss the real problems associated with racism.

Believe it our not, education and communication will start to bring a much clearer understanding of the different racial groups living in this country and abroad.

Thirdly, we must institute anti-racism education programs which involves expressing the destructiveness of racial prejudice. Learning racism is something people of color have had to live with all of their lives, so unlearning racism will not happen overnight.

Therefore, this process will probably take a few generations of de-programming and re-educating.

But in the meantime, the president, congress and all Federal and local government agencies and the Armed Forces must step forward now, begin denouncing racism and set up laws that will combat it throughout this country.

Since the United States is the world leader among nations and the melting pot for all races of people, we should be the leader in combating racial prejudice by using all of her power to eradicate it from her society. That is why it is very important that we elect politicians who have a conscious and who are compassionate enough to do what is right for all people and for the nation as a whole.

Personally speaking, If I were in the position of authority, I would call all leaders of the many different racial groups living in this country, and we would all sit down and meet to begin to talk out our many differences and problems that we face and then begin to work toward a better working relationship between ourselves.

Then, and only then, will we be able to say that we are making progress in the right direction which in turn brings about peace within this nation.

In order to prevent another incident like the Rodney King beating, our law enforcement agencies must begin to setup anti-racism campaigns, work shops and classes in all of their training programs. Consequently, all officers will have a clearer concept of people from different ethnic groups.

This will, in turn, probably ease the mistrust that people of color have for law enforcement officers because of individuals like the Mark Furhman's who disregard the law with their hatred of people and their interpretation of law and order. These people need to be stopped and removed from all law enforcement agencies and ultimately jailed. That is why it is very important that all agencies screen and re-screen all applicants before they are issued a badge.

Because if not, they become bad apples, and one bad apple will spoil the entire bunch with their slime of corruption, deceit, abuse, slurs, prejudice and hatred.

If all of our law enforcement agencies across the country would adhere to this advice, then society would not have so many Mark Furhmans walking around with badges.

Our schools and colleges must take the lead to become more involved in the process to re-educate our children. It is very vital that our schools and colleges have an anti-racism focus to combat the misconception and to give accurate knowledge about people of color.

Our schools and colleges are the center of knowledge and for that reason, they should become the center where anti-racism education begins. Parents and guardians must also play a vital role to ensure that our children are reared to respect one another and to have open minds and not to allow negative images portrayed by the media and society to cloud their judgments of people different from themselves.

For that reason, we must insist on realistic images and accurate information about people from different races and cultural backgrounds for the media and society. Because these are the ones who controls the television programs our children watch, the music our children listen to , the movies our children pay money to go and see.

For the time has come for us, as parents, teachers, church officials, neighbors, and others who are concerned, to take a stand against this injustice being done to our society.

Lastly, in conjunction with everything else, we need God's guidance and His spirit to bring us through this. In the Bible ...

2 Chronicles 7:14 says: *"If my people, which are called by my name, shall humble themselves, and pray and seek my face, and turn from their wicked ways, then will I hear from heaven, and will forgive their sin, and will heal their land ".*

Not only to heal the land but also heal the wounds caused by Racism. This is the cry of our children so that their world will be a peaceful, unified and equal place to live.

I stress that 'We' cannot and we must not leave God out of the healing process. If any thing is ever to be accomplished, we must rely on instruction from God. First we must humble ourselves before Him, pray and seek His face (seek His ways; love one another and do good to one another) and turn from our wicked ways, and He will heal our hearts and minds.

When racism is allowed to continue in the land, then the land is in trouble, in pain, wounded, beaten and bloody. For that reason, it is no good to anyone except the devil who loves destruction, division, hatred, and broken people. God is the only way to heal our land. So I close by saying, let us give God the chance to heal our land and each other.

Let us bound together in Love and heal our land by bringing an end to racism once and for all. It is up to us as a people, as a nation, as a society and especially builders of tomorrow. Because if there is ever to be a brighter or better tomorrow, we must start today to heal the Scars of Racism.

To God be the Glory of it All . God Bless You and Keep You All.

THE END

APPENDIX:

GO Deep and Not Cheap

The N - Word:

The foulest word in the English language or any language is the N - word. It is a word that dehumanizes and degrades African and African American people, those people of African decent. It strips one of their dignity and self worth. Commonly used by fearful ignorant and cowardly individuals who lack intelligence. So they use the N - word to try to degrade and purposely hurt African people simply because it is so easy to do.

It is easy to hurt than to love, hurting people different from yourself is so easy than trying to get to know and understand that person. For so long society has avoided trying to get to know people of different cultural and racial backgrounds.

In hurting people of African decent, the N - word come into play. As African people if we believe that we are less than nothing than the racist cowardly, ignorant, and fearful individuals win. So let us end once and for all the impact of the N-word.

Additional Information:
To research more information on Racism, I recommend reading the following books.

- **The Holy Bible**
  KJV*NIV*RSV

- **"How I Got Over"**
  Vol I & Vol II
  Colleen Birchett, Ph.D.

- **"Stony The Road We Trod"**
  Cain Hope Felder

- **"Roots"**
  Alex Haley

- **"The Timetables of African-American History"**
  Sharon Harley

- **"Where Do We Go From Here: Chaos or Community"**
  Dr. Martin Luther King, Jr.

- **The Black Presence in the Bible**
  Vol I & Vol II"
  Rev. Walter Arthur McCray

Additional Information:

To research more information on Racism, I recommend reading the following books.

- "Message to the Black Man in America"
  Elijah Muhammad

- "The African Cultural Heritage Topical
  Bible KJV - NIV"
  Pneuma Life Publishing

- "The Nehemiah Plan"
  Dr. Frank M. Reid, III

- "Experience And Tradition: A Primer In
  Black Biblical Hermeneutics"
  Stephen Breck Reid

- "Philosophy On Community Policing"

  "Identifying the Need For the Michigan
  Law Enforcement Officers Training
  Council to Change the Curriculum of the
  Basic Police Academy in Order to Address
  the Expectations of Today's Diverse
  Society"

(Available in Southfield Public Library)

Joseph E. Thomas, Jr.
Chief of Police
Southfield, Michigan

• "100 Amazing Facts on the African
  Presence in the Bible"
  Winston-Derek Publishing Communicator
  Press Project

Note: This list could go on and on because
there are more courageous writers who are
bringing down the walls of darkness. I
recommend that you read these books and
consult your local library for more
information.

I pray that this book has enlightened you and
that you will go forth and enlighten others on
the truth of the severeness of Racism.

Contributors:

⊕

Brother Ralph 2X:
Muhammad's Mosque of Islam No. 11
Boston, Massachusetts

42 years old; Married with 5 children; Postal
Clerk; Born and reared in Boston

Major Donald McClanahan:
Monroe Police Department
Monroe, Louisiana

49 years old; Been with the department for 27
years

Chief Joseph E. Thomas:
Southfield Police Department
Southfiled, Michigan

38 years old; Married, children

Rev. Virgil Vandenburg:
Pastor Emeritus & Teacher
Detroit, Michigan

80 years old; Married; 3 children; 54 years in
the ministry

Cardinal Chimba Chui:
Shrine of the Black Madonna Book Store
Pan-African Orthodox Christian Church
Detroit, Michigan

Rev. Michael Curry
Associate Minister
Hartford Memorial Baptist Church
Detroit, Michigan

Mother Sadie Adams:
Bethel Friendship Missionary Baptist Church
Highland Park, Michigan

Deacon Charles Johnson:
Bethel Friendship Missionary Baptist Church
Highland Park, Michigan

Married; 4 children; 3 Grandchildren

Evangelist Annie Babs:
Bethel Friendship Missionary Baptist Church
Highland Park, Michigan

47 years old; Mother of one; Church officer

Minister Eugene Hughes:
Logtown Baptist Church
Monroe, Louisiana

- ORDER FORM -

⊕ Rev. Christopher D. Handy
P.O. Box 323
Southfield, MI 48037-0323
(810) 356 - 1668

1. The Scars of Racism (Discovering
the meaning, cause and solutions to a problem that
plagues our society)

Name _____

Street Address _____

_____

City _____

1. The Scars of Racism __Copies x 12.99 ___

Shipping (Add $2.00 for 1 book = .50 for each addl.)

**TOTAL ENCLOSED (Check/M.O.,
payable to Rev. Christopher D. Handy) $_____**

Mail to:
Rev. Christopher D. Handy, P.O. Box 323,
Southfield, MI   48037-0323

- ORDER FORM -

⊕ Rev. Christopher D. Handy
P.O. Box 323
Southfield, MI 48037-0323
(810) 356 - 1668

1. **The Scars of Racism** (Discovering the meaning, cause and solutions to a problem that plagues our society)

Name _____

Street Address _____

_____

City _____

1. The Scars of Racism __Copies x 12.99 ___

Shipping (Add $2.00 for 1 book = .50 for each addl.)

**TOTAL ENCLOSED (Check/M.O.,
payable to Rev. Christopher D. Handy) $_____**

**Mail to:
Rev. Christopher D. Handy, P.O. Box 323,
Southfield, MI   48037-0323**